praise for PLEASURE

"Gary Young's finely wrought meditations are imagist poems that narrate the poet's embrace of all essence that sustains him: beautiful food, his family, especially his precocious son, his vision of the world as art and artifact. Each poem chronicles a treasured acceptance. Each one is like a fresh slice of melon."
—Diane Wakoski, author of *Emerald Ice: Selected Poems 1962–1987*

"Gary Young's prose poems are luminous miniatures, alert to every tremor of spirit that informs daily life. Quietly, simply, and brilliantly, they bring us into the presence of ordinary miracles. *Pleasure* is a book I savored, and wanted never to end."
—Kim Addonizio, author of *What Is This Thing Called Love* and *Little Beauties*

"In a time of great harm to the ordinary parts of our lives, Young finds the capacity to resist. He finds it in his embrace of his wife, his sons, nature's spare beauty, and the lingering delights of life. Take much from Young's *Pleasure;* much is generously offered. You'll find sustenance and grace."
—D. J. Waldie, author of *Holy Land: A Suburban Memoir*

praise for NO OTHER LIFE

"Gary Young has honed a sinuous, brief prose-poem form that carries a flavor uniquely its own—unflinching, stringent in beauty, austerely moving."
—Jane Hirshfield, author of *Given Sugar, Given Salt*
and *Each Happiness Ringed by Lions*

"Gary Young's project in *Braver Deeds* is to ask unsentimentally what a body's terms are, how much it can take. His answers are the more affecting for how formal he has had to make them. Loosen just a hair, his poems imply, and it won't seem worth it to go on."
—James McMichael, author of *Capacity* and *The World at Large*

"Transparent and refreshing, vital like the stream that flows through the 'insulating mist' of his canyon, Gary Young's beautiful *Days* flow on in elegant simplicity. This is a book Basho would admire."
—Sam Hamill, author of *Almost Paradise: Selected Poems & Translations*
and *Dumb Luck*

Also by Gary Young

No Other Life 2005
Braver Deeds 1999
Days 1997
The Dream of a Moral Life 1990
Hands 1979
The Geography of Home: California's Poetry of Place 1999
    (with Christopher Buckley)

Pleasure

POEMS *by* GARY YOUNG

Heyday Books · Berkeley, California

Library of Congress Cataloging-in-Publication Data
Young, Gary, 1951–
  Pleasure : poems / by Gary Young.
      p. cm.
  ISBN 1-59714-023-6 (pbk. : alk. paper)
  1. Prose poems, American. I. Title.
  PS3575.O785P57 2006
  811'.54--dc22

                                    2005022893

Designed by Gary Young
Cover design by Lorraine Rath
Author photograph by Jake Young
Printing and Binding: McNaughton & Gunn, Saline, MI

Orders, inquiries, and correspondence should be addressed to:
        Heyday Books
        P. O. Box 9145, Berkeley, CA 94709
        (510) 549-3564, Fax (510) 549-1889
        www.heydaybooks.com

Printed in the United States of America

10 9 8 7 6 5 4 3 2 1

For my family and friends—pure pleasure

ACKNOWLEDGMENTS

Grateful acknowledgment is made to the following magazines where these poems previously appeared: *Basalt, Cue: A Journal of Prose Poetry, Denver Quarterly, Double Room, Faultline, Flights, Heliotrope, Hotel Amerika, Hubbub, The Journal, The Kenyon Review, Luna, N.O.L.A. Spleen, Paragraph, Poetry International, Pool, Quarterly West, Quarter After Eight, Quick Fiction, Redactions, Redwood Coast Review, Sentence, Slope, Two Rivers Review, Tundra, Wild Strawberries.*

"My son was possessed," and "When I was a young man" appeared in *No Boundaries: Prose Poems by 24 American Poets,* Tupelo Press, Dorset, VT. "We buried Sarah's father" appeared in *Homage to Vallejo,* Greenhouse Review Press, Santa Cruz, CA. "The signature mark of autumn" appeared in *So Luminous the Wildflowers: an Anthology of California Poetry,* Tebot Bach, Huntington Beach, CA. Many of these poems appeared in *No Harm Done,* a limited edition from Sutton Hoo Press. "You write poems" appeared in a broadside printed by Felicia Rice and Ruth McGurk for the Center for Book Arts, New York, NY. "Stephen marinated salmon" appeared in a broadside from Heyday Books for the Wild Salmon Festival.

I would like to thank the National Endowment for the Arts for a fellowship grant, and the Ucross Foundation for a residency, which helped with the completion of this book. – G. Y.

"The Vedas tell us" is for Michael Hannon.
"Stephen marinated salmon" is for Stephen Kessler.
"We'd been talking" is for Ray Gonzalez.
"A warm current" is for Brad Crenshaw.
"She handed me a piece of salmon" is for Jennifer Clarke and Paul Hansen.
"We bought halibut" is for Killarney Clary.
"When I step in from the deck" is for Christopher Buckley.

I'm grateful to the many friends who read earlier versions of these poems, especially Killarney Clary, Stephen Kessler and Christopher Buckley.

CONTENTS

"Pleasure lies in being, not becoming."

THOMAS AQUINAS

It's a joy to be subtracted from the world. Holding my son's naked body against my own, all I feel is what he is. I cannot feel my own skin. I cannot feel myself touching him, but I can recognize his hair, the heft of his body, his warmth, his weight. I cannot measure my own being, my subtle boundaries, but I know my son's arms, the drape of his legs, smooth and warm in a shape I can measure. I have become such a fine thing, the resting-place for a body I can know.

The Vedas tell us that human perfection is achieved only in dreamless sleep; no desire, no fear, no ego, just a state of pure being. I believe that's true, but waking from a dream to rain drumming the windows and the roof, I draw my legs across the warm cotton sheets, bury my head in the pillows and rest this side of sleep; no longing, no anxiety, no harm done.

A tall man in a white apron and a starched white shirt stands at a table folding napkins. There's a bowl of sliced lemons on the counter; I can smell them. Light seems to pour from the walls. My wife turns to me and says, I love you. She's pleased with herself; she found this place. A bouquet of tulips is reflected in a mirror behind the bar, and so are we. There's a song on the radio I've never heard before—you can't kill me because I'm already dead.

I stood on a narrow bridge where the marsh meets the incoming tide, and I saw two birds. The first one called out softly as it turned and drifted on the wind, while the other one, made of light, slid silently over the surface of the bay.

Three women walked toward me on the street, and all of them were lovely, but one was more beautiful than the rest. Her breasts, loose under a gauzy blouse, swayed with every step, and her nipples carved little circles in the air. As she was about to pass me she dropped her keys, and stopped just an arm's length away. Before I could move, she bent over from the waist, and out of modesty, or courtesy, I might have turned away, but I looked.

I couldn't find the mushrooms under the begonias in the garden, then I remembered I had seen them growing there in a dream. The flowering thistle, dewdrops clinging to the spider's web—it wasn't all a dream. That's coffee I smell, not wood smoke; and here's the glass vial where my wife has saved all our children's teeth.

Stephen marinated salmon in garlic, ginger, sesame oil and lime. He fired oak bark in a small iron kettle, and when the coals were the color of the fish, he laid the salmon skin-side down on the tiny grill. The cry of sea lions carried up the ridge on a breeze. Below us, the garden was bolting; a head of lettuce lay withered from the heat, but we picked another. We slipped the salmon from the grill, and ate it while the sea turned orange, then purple, and finally disappeared. A hawk circled overhead, and in the fading light I watched the dead limbs of a tree shaped like a man running from crown to crown across the sky.

Since dawn, the dove's melancholic repetitions have haunted the air. Melodies from childhood, oh, please not that. Some memories I can feel in my body like a bruise. Mothers walk by with their little ones, and the dove keeps singing. A mockingbird starts up on a branch nearby: it's call and response—the pitiful piping of the dove, and the giddy exuberance of the mocker. Their music is a clairvoyance. Who knew I'd be whistling by now? Who could have guessed I'd be singing such a happy song?

I took my son into the forest. He is a fearless child, but he was frightened by the woods and never left my side. We found chanterelles under the oaks, and carried them home for dinner. Even in the kitchen my son clung to me. We cooked the mushrooms with a handful of garlic in olive oil and butter. I added chicken, seven lemons, seven limes, and a scoop of cinnamon, why not? Steam from the noodles fogged our windows, so the moon that night was vague, mysterious, but available.

When I was a young man and found I had cancer, my friends held a benefit. There was music and dancing, and when the night was over, they gave me a paper bag filled with cash. My wife then was always worried about money, but whenever she panicked, I reached into the sack and handed her a fistful of bills. I'll never be that rich again. Not a moment escaped me. I had everything I needed and nothing to lose. I've never been happier than when I was dying.

My brother's been reading the *Diagnostic and Statistical Manual of Mental Disorders*. It's 1,200 pages, he says, and he says, I've been thinking, if they gave everyone a hundred thousand dollars that manual would only be nine pages long. You'd have a little psychosis, a little depression, a little post-traumatic stress, and that's about all. One hundred thousand dollars, he says; I'd be happy just to sell my truck.

A warm current moved up the coast and brought albacore to our cold waters. I bought a whole tuna at the docks, and took the fish back to my home in the mountains. It was winter, but Brad wanted to cook outside, so we stood in the rain smoking cigars under umbrellas held high above the fire. We grilled the fish in a crust of ginger, lemongrass, cayenne and basil, but we left the meat raw inside and drizzled it at the table with lemon juice, wasabi and soy. While we ate, the rain turned to slush, and long before we had finished, the fire beneath the metal grill sputtered, steamed and went out.

The boys have no idea how beautiful they are, and this, of course, makes them lovelier. They jog in loose formation. They stretch and run and never tire. Their uniforms, bloodied where a steel cleat has caught an ankle, or grass-stained and streaked with dirt after a hard slide, cannot camouflage their sadness or their splendor. They are so lonesome in their bodies.

An owl called out from the orchard, and I called back. Three more owls hooted, and together we began a chorus. Later that night, my son woke up when I kissed him in his bed. He wanted a story, and I told him about the cold, about the owls and the footsteps I'd made in the snow he didn't know had fallen. He wouldn't sleep until I promised to show him in the morning, and in the morning, though it was quiet, he could see the footprints were still there.

The signature mark of autumn has arrived at last with the rains: orange of pumpkin, orange persimmon, orange lichen on rocks and fallen logs; a copper moon hung low over the orchard; moist, ruddy limbs of the madrone, russet oak leaf, storm-peeled redwood, acorns emptied by squirrels and jays; and mushrooms, orange boletes, Witch's Butter sprouting on rotted oak, the Deadly Galeria, and of course, chanterelles, which we'll eat tonight with pasta, goat cheese, and wine.

My son was possessed by the Devil. Beelzebub had entered his body and distorted his tiny features. His face was red and twisted. He gnashed his teeth, and struggled in my arms. I rapped his forehead with two fingers to drive the demon from his body, and woke up shouting, *get out, get out.* I lay in bed and listened to my wife's heavy breathing. I could hear the boy calling softly in his sleep. A hard rain fell steadily against the metal gutters, then it stopped.

A full moon rises over the orchard where two owls sit perched on a snow-dusted tree. One owl falls forward, and floats toward me with wings spread wide, my cold heart moving on.

We buried Sarah's father in the cemetery on Meder Street. He had told his daughter, I'll be dead in three days, and three days later he was—a Thursday without clouds, the year 5762 by his count, but he's past all calculation now. That afternoon we listened to an ancient music: the mourner's Kaddish, the rustle of leaves, and hard earth falling on a casket. It was getting hot; the wind had fallen out of the trees. I stopped at the grave of my old friend Zwerling who once ground the lenses for my glasses in a shed behind his shop. I set a piece of honey-colored marble on one side of his tombstone. On the other side there were other stones—a flat river rock, scraps of granite, a black stone, a white one.

My son says, I wish I could be in my body. You are in your body, I tell him. No, he says, I'm in my self. Only my self, he says, and shakes his head. I wish I could be in my body, he says, and he walks away tapping one hand lightly against his thigh.

Stephen sends me clippings from the *Times*. Joe Black, a pitcher for the Dodgers, is dead. The poet Philip Whalen is dead. A Buddhist Lama, dead for 80 years, sits in a full lotus dressed in a golden robe, his radiant skin still pliant. In Montana, a desperate man feeds a boy to his neighbors; in the New Square Fish Market a 20-pound carp shouts apocalyptic warnings in Hebrew. We can't resist, and though we spend our whole lives trying, can never touch all there is.

In a small pool surrounded by trees, my son is learning to swim. A woman kneels beside him in the water. He's on his back, arms at his side, and the woman holds him up with a single hand. She leans forward, whispers slowly, and when she feels his body relax, she pulls her hand away and he floats there, unaware of what he's done.

We'd been talking about the limits of our resolve, and I admitted that sometimes I resent my own life. Of course my resentment always turns to longing, I said, and I'm filled with the wonder of my existence. Then I think about death, how it offends me, and how I love this life so much I could die of it, and my resentment begins again. While we spoke, a hummingbird hovered above the stream; how hard they both worked, moving constantly just to stay in place.

For three days the menacing silence of a child's empty room; no hum of jets flying low over the mountains, no ropy contrails crossing the sky above the bay. A thousand conversations end in mid-sentence, and we wish we could hold our breath forever; but today is the birthday of the world, and everything must begin again. My son puts a tiny finger to his lips and says, hush, someone's sleeping, an angel.

I carried my mother's ashes home and set them on a shelf. I couldn't save her. Ten years passed, and another ten years. Turning fifty, I am older now than my mother ever was, and she has become my sweet child at last.

I woke in panic from a terrifying dream. A rosebush in bloom
beside the broken pane of a greenhouse window still lingered in
my mind, and I remembered that as I was falling asleep you
crawled into bed beside me. Your mother said, Daddy isn't well,
and you pulled your fingers across my face. I held you there as
long as I could, my hand on your back where I could feel your
heart, relentless in its cage of bone.

Weeks past the solstice, rain lingering day after day, I gave up on spring, and surrendered to the sullen sky. To think I almost turned a deaf ear to heaven. Last night, in a lull between storms, the ruinous orchard bloomed in secret, and this morning there is a fragrance in the air like music.

There was a total eclipse of the sun, and the light at the beach turned vaporous. The air chilled quickly, the wind picked up, and in the weakening light a young woman left her friends at the shoreline and walked toward me. She smiled, held a straw hat up to my chest and said, look. Sunlight passed through the tiny spaces in the weave, and I was covered with dozens of tiny suns, all shrinking to slivers against my skin as the moon slid silently above.

My son stepped between two mirrors positioned to reveal an endless train of reflections stretching to infinity. When he looked at the string of his reflections left and right, I expected him to laugh, but he said, come home, all you children, come home.

She handed me a piece of salmon, ruby-hued and redolent of wood smoke and the sea. Moist, silky with oil, I ate the fish slowly, and told her, I've only eaten salmon like this once, years ago on the Skagit River. She said, this salmon was caught on the Skagit. She went on, but I wasn't listening. I was thinking of eagles in the cedars; raw oysters, fennel bread, salmon and white wine; oyster shells in the middens; ice breaking under our boots on the trail to Fishtown.

My son has drawn two circles, two faces on the asphalt in chalk. He's given each face a nose, and their mouths, two wavy lines, are smiling. My son has made two dim marks on one of the faces, and he tells me, this one can't see because his eyes are too small. I say, that's very sad, but my son says, it's all right, because his friend—whose eyes are slashes of color that dance across his face like flames—sees very, very well.

We bought halibut fresh from the boat, and poached the firm white flesh with onions, fennel root and wine. We mashed potatoes, nibbled jicama, and Killarney laughed because the meal was white. She's written a book about her mother, and that night I decided to illustrate the book with clouds.

There wasn't flesh enough to resist the syringe, so I'd drive it in as far as I dared and release the morphine. Her body would stiffen, then relax; she'd catch her breath and release a string of sighs as if she were coming. There was something we could do. It wasn't all a horror.

I rose before dawn, and watched a small cloud blush as the sun began to rise. My wife and my children kept sleeping, and I had the quiet house to myself. I let the cat in through the front door, and out again through the back. I read in silence. This once was all my life, poems and silence, cutting woodblocks and pulling prints in my studio day after day. I loved it, but not enough to live alone. No footfalls, no shouts, no one crying out for me in the night; no, I could never have lived without the others to forgive me.

Two ravens call from a redwood after the storm. Two black stones, they skip from one branch to another, and when they do, raindrops catch the failing light, and a shower of sparks falls from every stricken tree.

My son fell asleep beside me on the bed. I slept too, and later, woke up dizzy, almost sick with happiness. My son's warm breath was all around me in the room, and his small bones rested there with mine.

Every Wednesday, Fidel brings oysters to the market. I like to eat them with salsa, cilantro and lime. I like to run my tongue along the slick lip of the inner shell and suck them into my mouth. I love knowing they're alive. Fidel wants to know, how many? And when I tell him, I'll start with two, he taps his blunt knife against a block of ice, and shucks three.

Hunting mushrooms under the pine trees, I bend and brush needles from the brassy helmets of the dead.

The swallows hide their children in the dark, in frail mud cups beneath the roof. They fly from the house and come back. They make loops in the treacherous air, then return. They live here, too, and they're not afraid.

It's early winter, and the begonias have delivered a second bloom. Scarlet blossoms hang heavily from their brittle stems; peach-hued blossoms as large as my head mingle with yellow ones, orange, apricot and pink. The annual beds are still an embarrassing spectacle of color—cyclamen, azaleas, even a lily has held off its bloom until now. I step down the stone walk toward the house, absorbed in the dazzle of the garden, and the hummingbird that hectored me all summer when I watered spins just inches before my face. I stumble on the brick walk, and the small bird hovers over me for a long moment, then swings back home, its crimson head chattering.

I was searching my notebook for the line to a poem, and I found: the crows fly out to sea at dusk, and nest each night on the moon. On the facing page, there's a recipe: blend a clove of garlic, kalamata olives, a tablespoon of capers.

Near Santa Maria, a large, purple deer ran onto the highway, then dissolved in a shimmering cascade of light. I'd fallen asleep driving, and that dazzling animal woke me. Thirty years later, passing the same spot just south of the river, my wife beside me, my children nestled in the back seat, I couldn't count the miracles that have brought us this far.

I left home when I was seventeen. Seventeen years later you and I were married, and today we have been married for seventeen years. It's a queer calculus. For seventeen years I have turned to you in the dark, and teased your nipples with my tongue. I have watched your body swell with children, and I have seen our children slip startled and wide-eyed into the world. There is a locust that rises from the ground only once every seventeen years. When the time comes, bury me deep. It's only love that's held me here this long, and even in the grave I'll still want you in my bones.

I know that bird calling out in the night. This isn't the first time he's mistaken moonlight for sunrise.

The beans soaking in the steel pot had the luster of polished stones. While they simmered, I sautéed onions, garlic, tomatoes and leeks. There was basil at the bottom of the jar, so I added that, and rubbed a stem of thyme between my palms and let it fall. The kitchen was moist and warm, and the windows steamed over as if curtains had been drawn. When the soup was ready, I lifted a spoonful to my mouth, and before I took a sip, closed my eyes the way I do when I'm about to kiss.

Who would volunteer to live any moment more than once? I might. This morning I smelled freesias in the garden and closed my eyes. Suddenly I was young again, and you were still alive.

There was something in the air I couldn't place. I recognized the musky sage, alfalfa, fragrance of rain rising from the muddy road, and ozone after the storm had passed. There was a trace of leather, of damp wood, mold and stale tobacco, and a fugitive scent carried on the cries of the birds—I could smell the humming leaves that quivered in the branches of the cottonwood.

When I step in from the deck after smoking a cigar, my wife glares at me and says, you stink—but I can't resist. They punctuate the routine drudgery of a day, and not with a comma, but an exclamation point, a smoky ellipsis of desire . . . . *Robusto, torpedo, maduro:* we need a Romance language to talk about cigars. Buckley once handed me a fat Cubano, a *Romeo y Julieta* made in a factory where a worker reads poetry aloud while the others roll. I could taste the difference. A cigar is never just a cigar; it's a wet kiss, a tongue in your mouth, and both of you burning.

The world cannot be contained. This morning I saw a mockingbird catch a butterfly in mid-air, and with the bright wings fluttering in its beak, it seemed to burst into blossom.

On the nights I can't sleep, I try to think of the people who comfort me, and the landscapes that I love. I try to imagine thunderheads over the prairie, cottonwoods and a certain stream, but it's like thinking about my body: each time I come back, I fear it's for the last time. I fall asleep at last by telling myself I'll do anything I can to return.

The poet is barely visible in the tiny hut suspended over the gorge. He's small, but not insignificant: he's the one who held the brush and made this landscape. There are real ravines, green, green as ink.

The scent of wild azalea eddies in the breeze. Purple blossoms fall from the catalpas, and petals rain down from the wisteria that has climbed into the highest branches of a tree. The soft air filled with dying breath is sweet.

While I was away it seemed another world, not this one where your breath charms the air I breathe in sleep. I was gone too long; let's embrace regret, and love the world. I brought you a story— in the city, there were yellow leaves in a whirlwind that followed me down a cobbled street.

My brother will tell you, trout only stop feeding when there's nothing to eat, so he fishes all year long. In mid-winter he'll break through the ice on a stream in Wyoming, and dapple the open water with a bead-headed streamer. Setting his waders against an icy bank, he'll cast into an open riffle, and barely mend his line before a slender, ravenous fish clears the water, hovers there, spins, and splinters the light, falls and slides over the frozen surface of the stream, the hook set firmly in its mouth.

Jack is telling a joke at the bar. He begins, two guys are out hunting, and when he's finished, everybody laughs. John shows up and Jack repeats the joke, then Rick arrives, and John says, let me tell him. A guy rides into town on a horse, he says. No, wait, it's a beautician, I don't remember, it doesn't matter, it will come to me, he says, and goes on. They told that joke all night, and I laughed out loud each time.

When I was a boy, I hunted fossils in the badlands. I wandered the washes and the gullies with my head down, not looking, but waiting for a glint of bone, or the bright enamel of a half-buried tooth. Thirty years later, digging a trench, I reached into a shovelful of earth, and before I realized I'd stopped digging, I held the sharp incisor of a grizzly. I hadn't seen the tooth until I held it in my hand, but for a moment I'd found my skillful child's eye, a grace I thought I'd lost.

Michael and I take an airplane to Hong Kong. We go to an outdoor market and watch a man stir-frying beans. There are fruits, spices, hot peppers and bright vegetables hung on poles supporting the tents in the marketplace. When it's time to leave, we walk through customs. Michael turns to me and asks, are we home? The customs agent motions us to step aside. He's suspicious, and I wonder if he knows that Michael is dead. The agent cocks his head at Michael and says, no luggage?

The fragrance welling up from the petals of the iris is more arousing than a woman's scent. This sexual vertigo is sadly charming; I would penetrate those petals if I could.

A woman kneeling at our table began to tell a story. It was my birthday, she said, I was ten, and I rode my new bike through a pasture on a dare. I was almost across when a bull charged from the far side of the field. I climbed a fence just in time, but the bull made a wreck of my bike. She paused, and I could see that her neck was much whiter than her shoulders or her face—I suppose her hair had just been cut. It's strange, she said, the things you never forget.

She cut the salmon so thin the light passed through, then she wrapped the fish around sticky balls of rice. She sliced an avocado, and spread two slivers at the end of each piece like petals on a tropical flower. She filled the other end with flying fish roe, orange, iridescent, and she separated the two pieces with a feathery spike of lemon. It was beautiful, everyone at the bar was staring, and the chef's simpleminded brother stopped mumbling to himself, rose from his stool in a corner of the kitchen, and applauded.

Exhausted by the day, and late to bed, we were eager for sleep, but grazed each other, carelessly—a single caress, and we were making love with such ferocity that I understood for the first time why they once called this dying; you came again and again, and I fell deeper inside you, past darkness, past time and all the world, then it was morning.

I bought eggplants at the farmer's market, long and slender, the deep purple reserved for nightshade, castor, the garden's poisonous brood. I was admiring the eggplant's waxy skin, its tender flesh, when a farmer thrust a tomato into my hand. I bit into the firm, red fruit, belladonna's passionate cousin, and ate it under his watchful eye. He looked at me and nodded, as if he knew how far I'd go for pleasure.

Every winter, I climb the apple tree to prune the deadwood and the suckers. I cut the dense, brittle limbs that have sloughed their bark, and let them fall. Below me, my son has gathered all the clippings, and stacked them in a pile. Someday I would like to lie down on a bed of apple boughs like that, and leave this earth as sweet, sweet smoke, but not yet.

He says, you write poems about what you see: trees, clouds, the mailbox, and me, Cooper.

It's a luxury to worry about our lives. A smoky haze was reported east of town. A dog was tied up and very hot. Someone ran over a mailbox, and a rubber raft was abandoned on the wetlands. A woman reported that she could hear children screaming and crying, but the children, of course, were only playing.

The shallow stream murmurs in its narrow bed. A wren repeats his signature riff, and redwoods groan in a stiffening breeze. Graffiti on the wall outside says, *I am Valentino Rossi, but not much else.* The world is a gift, a wedding. A woman wipes juice from her child's sticky lips. Someone says, I collect maps. The frozen bolt gives way at last.

I took the children to pick berries, and their fingers and their faces were soon stained red with warm, sweet juice. There were mice running ahead of the children in the furrows, and overhead there were hawks, waiting for them.

When my wife arrived, I was waving a wooden spoon above my head, and dancing, wearing nothing but a towel. It was eight o'clock, warm and still light, even under the redwoods. That morning I'd set four large stones—the last stones in the last wall—and later, I finished framing the guesthouse. That afternoon I folded laundry, cleaned the toilets and caught a gopher in the flower bed; the day went on and on. Chicken with wild mushrooms was heating in the oven. Tracy Nelson was on the stereo singing *Every Night of the Week*. The boys sat naked on the couch, and at last, I dished out dinner, still in my towel.

A sparrow preens its wings on a power line overhead, and casts a filmy shadow across the dusty road, a charcoal drawing erased and redrawn each time the sparrow shudders or twists. The world is reinvented endlessly.

The roads were closed, and the power was out for six days after the storm. I tried to work by lantern light, but what's the use? There was plenty of wine, and after two days, the food in the freezer began to thaw, so we cooked it all. We fed the neighbors chicken with garlic, then herbed sausage with wild rice and beans. We ate by candlelight, and every meal tasted better than the one before. We emptied the pantry, but there were potatoes, a pound of mushrooms, and the last of the raspberries floating in the cooler when a friend walked in with a dripping bag, and said, how do you want to cook this lamb?

Brad's patient lives in a counterfeit world. He drives a car identical to his own, but it's not his car. He lives in a replica of his real house, and he knows that the man who pretends to be his son is not his son. He's resigned to this world. He no longer asks his wife, what have you done with my wife? But his life still troubles him. There's one thing I can't understand, he says. And he asks Brad—who would go to so much trouble?

My son and I were standing on a large rock at the shoreline. The sun had set, and twilight glazed the breakers and the backwash. The tide was rising, and a wave broke around the rock and surrounded it. My wife called out, come back, but my son said, don't worry, I dreamed about this; I know what will happen. And while my wife ran back and forth on the wet sand, my son and I waltzed on our own tiny island.

I walked into the hills, to the top of a butte, and found the center of the world. A hawk circled overhead, and a shallow stream etched a thin, blue line into the canyon below. I sat down beside a fossil leaf embedded in a flat, red stone, poised, for an instant, between time and eternity.

Elizabeth fed me—pasta with anchovies, lentils with sage—
always a different dish. Gene talked: about love nests, the prairie
in winter, and how once, as a child, he'd determined he was God.
We sat at a table and looked out at a gingko and a locust, and in
spring, a crab apple blossomed beneath the upstairs window.
There were paintings on every wall, ceramics on every shelf, and
flowers—orchids, zinnias, asters. Elizabeth once made a salad with
spinach, walnuts, blue cheese and pear. Then she picked a daylily
from a bouquet on the counter, chopped it and sprinkled it over
the greens. We spent years that way, feasting on the world.

Acrobats vanished behind a veil of thick, blue smoke. Jugglers tossed hatchets and knives, but it was hot, my son was restless, and we wandered out to the deserted midway. My son ran between the empty amusements while a loudspeaker blared, come see the world's smallest horse. I could hear the animal whinny from its stall while the disembodied voice called, come on over, come on in, this is something that you'll never see again. My son pushed his way through a padlocked gate and was too excited to answer when I called him back, or perhaps he couldn't hear me over the tape's continuous loop crying, he's alive, he's alive, he's alive.

At this hour I like to imagine that everyone I love is sleeping. There may be someone walking through a cold house, a mother up to quiet a restless child, drinking a glass of water, or reading in bed, unable to sleep. I know that somewhere the sun is shining, that people are busy at work or struggling, dying, but here, in the dark, I can imagine everyone at peace, in deep slumber, and it pleases me to think of them that way.

The world is at home in my mind. I can spell *Detroit*. I know where my cats are buried in the orchard. I know the quadratic equation, my mother's maiden name and the suicide squeeze. I know all the words to *A Good Woman's Love* and I can hear them in my head at will. Every thought is like a sweet rolled over the tongue. Even my bad ideas are good.

I'd like to reduce everything to one syllable—a groan, a sigh or startled come-cry. I'd like to hold the world in my mouth. I was looking for a single word, and the word was *you*.

Gary Young has been awarded grants from the National Endowment for the Humanities, the Vogelstein Foundation, and the California Arts Council. He has received a Pushcart Prize, twice won grants from the National Endowment for the Arts, and his book of poems, *The Dream of a Moral Life,* won the James D. Phelan Award. He is the author of several other collections of poetry including *Hands, Braver Deeds,* winner of the Peregrine Smith Poetry Prize, and *No Other Life,* which won the 2003 William Carlos Williams Award. He edits the Greenhouse Review Press and is a well-known printer and book artist whose work is represented in numerous collections including the Museum of Modern Art, the Victoria and Albert Museum and The Getty Center for the Arts. He lives with his wife and two sons in the mountains north of Santa Cruz, California.

HEYDAY INSTITUTE

Since its founding in 1974, Heyday Books has occupied a unique niche in the publishing world, specializing in books that foster an understanding of California history, literature, art, environment, social issues, and culture. We are a 501(c)(3) nonprofit organization based in Berkeley, California, serving a wide range of people and audiences throughout California and beyond. Our commitment is to enhance California's rich cultural heritage by providing a platform for writers, poets, artists, scholars, and storytellers who help keep this diverse legacy alive.

We are grateful for the generous funding we've received for our publications and programs during the past year from foundations and more than 300 individuals. Major recent supporters include:

Anonymous; Arroyo Fund; Bay Tree Fund; California Association of Resource Conservation Districts; California Oak Foundation; Candelaria Fund; CANfit; Columbia Foundation; Colusa Indian Community Council; Flow Fund Circle; Wallace Alexander Gerbode Foundation; Richard and Rhoda Goldman Fund; Evelyn & Walter Haas, Jr. Fund; Walter & Elise Haas Fund; Hopland Band of Pomo Indians; James Irvine Foundation; Guy Lampard; Jeff Lustig; George Fredrick Jewett Foundation; LEF Foundation; David Mas Masumoto; James McClatchy; Michael McCone; Gordon and Betty Moore Foundation; Morongo Band of Mission Indians; National Endowment for the Arts; National Park Service; Ed Penhoet; Rim of the World Interpretive Association; Riverside/San Bernardino County Indian Health; River Rock Casino; Alan Rosenus; John-Austin Saviano/Moore Foundation; Sandy Cold Shapero; Ernest and June Siva; LJ and Mary Skaggs Foundation; Strong Foundation for Environmental Values; Swinerton Family Fund; and the Harold and Alma White Memorial Fund.

For more information about Heyday Institute, our publications and programs, please visit our website at www.heydaybooks.com.